KU-062-537

grade 6

For full details of exam requirements, please refer to the current syllabus in conjunction with *Examination Information & Regulations* and the guide for candidates, teachers and parents, *These Music Exams*. These three documents are available online at www.abrsm.org, as well as free of charge from music retailers, from ABRSM local representatives or from the Services Department, The Associated Board of the Royal Schools of Music, 24 Portland Place, London W1B 1LU, United Kingdom.

CONTENTS

Where appropriate, pieces in this album have been checked with original source material and edited as necessary for instructional purposes. Any editorial additions to the texts are given in small print, within square brackets, or – in the case of slurs and ties – in the form ⁀. Fingering, metronome marks and the editorial realization of ornaments (where given) are for guidance only; they are not comprehensive or obligatory.

Editor for the Associated Board: **Richard Jones**

DO NOT PHOTOCOPY © MUSIC

Alternative pieces for this grade

© 2008 by The Associated Board of the Royal Schools of Music

No part of this publication may be copied or reproduced in any form or by any means without the prior permission of the publisher.

Music origination by Barnes Music Engraving Ltd
Cover by Økvik Design
Printed in England by Headley Brothers Ltd,
The Invicta Press, Ashford, Kent

A:1

Les petits moulins à vent

from 17e ordre, *Troisième livre de pièces de clavecin*

F. COUPERIN

The French composer, harpsichordist and organist François Couperin (1668–1733), the most distinguished of the Couperin family of musicians, was appointed organist at St Gervais in Paris on his 18th birthday and *organiste du roi* at the royal chapel seven years later, in 1693. He became the leading French harpsichord player-composer of his day, being awarded the title *maître de clavecin du roi* in 1717. Couperin published four books of harpsichord music, containing in all 27 *ordres* or suites. The individual movements are mostly character pieces whose source of inspiration is revealed in their titles. Wilfrid Mellers says of 'Les petits moulins à vent' (The Little Windmills) that it 'naturalistically imitates windmills, while giving them a human dimension in the form of idle chatterboxes'. The commas are Couperin's own marks of articulation; they denote a clean break between phrases, effected by lifting the fingers from the keys. Dynamics are left to the player's discretion.
Source: *Troisième livre de pièces de clavecin* (Paris, 1722)

A:2

Courante

Third movement from Suite in C, K. 399/385i

MOZART

In a letter to his sister Nannerl of 20 April 1782 Mozart said: 'The Baron van Swieten, to whom I go every Sunday, gave me all the works of Handel and Sebastian Bach to take home with me, after I had played them to him.' One result of this encounter with the great masters of the early 18th century was Mozart's imitation of Handel in the unfinished Suite in C (only the first three movements were completed), from which this Courante is drawn. Dynamics are left to the player's discretion.

Sources: autograph MS, microfilm, Internationale Stiftung Mozarteum, Salzburg; first edition, *Oeuvres complettes de W. A. Mozart, Cahier VI* (Leipzig: Breitkopf & Härtel, 1799)

Reproduced from Mozart: *Mature Piano Pieces*, edited by Richard Jones (ABRSM Publishing)

A:3

Sonata in D minor

Kp. 9

D. SCARLATTI

Domenico Scarlatti (1685–1757), Neapolitan by birth, emigrated to Portugal in around 1723, and then to Spain in 1729, spending the rest of his life at the Spanish court. The Sonata in D minor, Kp. 9, is the ninth of the 30 sonatas that make up his first published collection of harpsichord music, the *Essercizi* of 1738. In the preface Scarlatti wrote: 'In these compositions, do not expect any profound learning, but rather an ingenious jesting with art.' Dynamics are left to the player's discretion.

Source: *Essercizi per gravicembalo* (London, 1738)

Adagio

Second movement from Sonata in C, WoO 51

Edited by
Harold Craxton

BEETHOVEN

The Sonata in C, WoO 51, from which this Adagio is drawn, was composed in the 1790s. It was dedicated to Eleonore von Breuning, whom Beethoven had known since his childhood in Bonn and who later married Beethoven's friend Franz Wegeler. The young Beethoven's relations with the von Breuning family were later recalled by Wegeler: 'Soon he was treated as one of the children in the family, spending in the house not only the greater part of his days, but also many nights.' The end of the Adagio is missing in the autograph manuscript. The completion printed here (b. 26 onwards) is partly by Beethoven's pupil Ferdinand Ries and partly by Donald Francis Tovey, who was responsible for the last six bars.

Moderato

CHOPIN

Nineteenth-century composers often wrote short piano pieces in the albums of their patrons, friends or pupils. One such piece is this Moderato by Fryderyk Chopin (1810–49), which he wrote in 1843 in the album of Countess Anna de Cheremetieff. The piece was not published until 1910, over 60 years after the composer's death, when it appeared under the title 'Albumblatt' (Album Leaf). Where the hands cross, the player is left to decide which hand should go over the other.

Adapted from Chopin: *An Introductory Album* (ABRSM Publishing)

B:3

Molto tranquillo, semplice

No. 1 from *Three Little Piano Pieces*

STENHAMMAR

The Swedish composer Wilhelm Stenhammar (1871–1927) was active both as a concert pianist and as a conductor, working alongside Nielsen and Sibelius. His own music is late Romantic in style, but also incorporates elements derived from Scandinavian folk music. The first of his *Three Little Piano Pieces*, reproduced here, has the melodic charm and simplicity lf folk music, allied to a Brahmsian richness of piano sonority.

The Buccaneer

from *Eight Children's Pieces*, Op. 36

M. ARNOLD

The English composer Sir Malcolm Arnold (1921–2006) studied under Gordon Jacob at the Royal College of Music, and in the 1940s played trumpet in the London Philharmonic Orchestra. After a period of further study in Italy in 1948–9, he devoted himself entirely to composition. 'The Buccaneer' gives a vivid musical portrait of a swashbuckling pirate.

Reproduced by permission of Universal Music Publishing MGB Ltd. All enquiries about this piece, apart from those directly relating to the exams, should be addressed to Universal Music Publishing MGB Ltd, 20 Fulham Broadway, London SW6 1AH.

C:2

Jazz Exercise No. 2

from *Jazz Piano for the Young Pianist*, Vol. 3

O. PETERSON

The Canadian jazz pianist and composer Oscar Peterson (1925–2007) formed a trio for piano, guitar and double bass in the early 1950s, began to perform regularly as a solo pianist in the early 1970s, and over the years appeared with many of the foremost jazz musicians of the 20th century, including Ella Fitzgerald, Stan Getz, Dizzie Gillespie and Billie Holiday. Also active in the field of music education, he published a series entitled *Jazz Piano for the Young Pianist*, which includes exercises, minuets, etudes and pieces designed to help beginners develop a secure jazz technique.

Gnossienne No. 3

C:3

Lent [♩ = *c*.92]

SATIE

conseillez-vous soigneusement [consider carefully]

munissez-vous de clairvoyance
[be clear-sighted]

seul, pendant un instant [alone for a moment]

de manière à obtenir un creux
[strive for a hollow effect]

The French composer Erik Satie (1866–1925) studied at the Paris Conservatoire, and from 1888 became a regular pianist at Le Chat Noir cabaret in Montmartre. The six *Gnossiennes* are among his early works, dating from 1889–97. The title is a word invented by Satie as an evocation (it is believed) of the ritual dances performed in the ancient Cretan city of Gnossos (Knossos). The somewhat eccentric performance instructions are typical of the composer and need not be taken too literally. Accidentals apply only to the note they precede and to any consecutive notes at the same pitch.

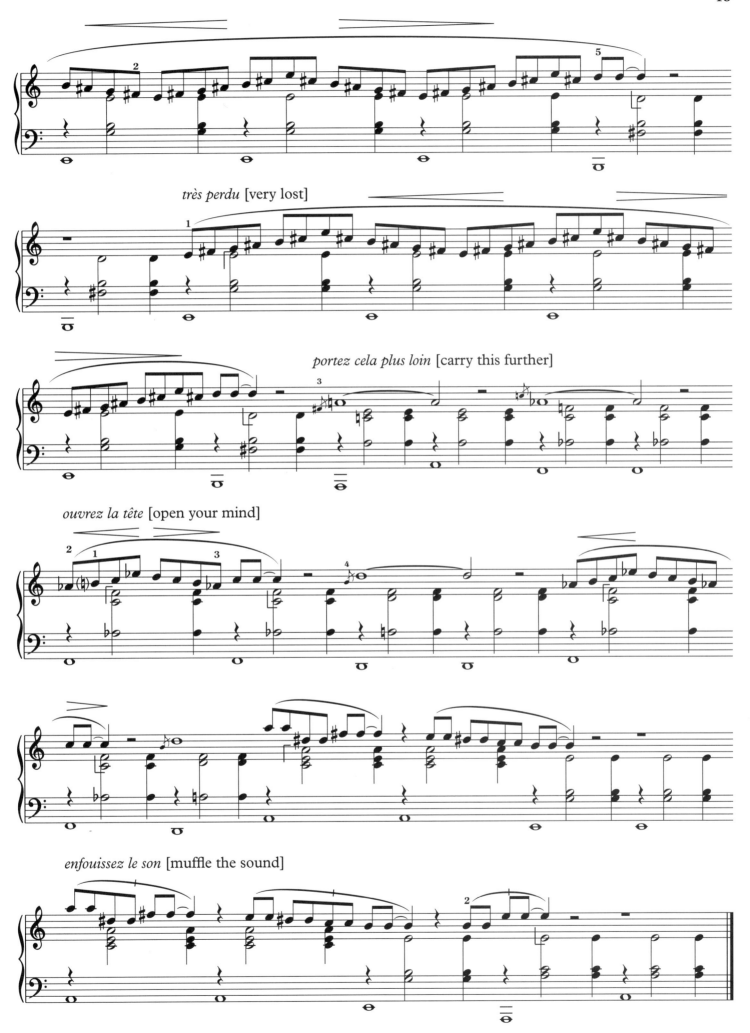

très perdu [very lost]

portez cela plus loin [carry this further]

ouvrez la tête [open your mind]

enfouissez le son [muffle the sound]